His Beauty

For

My Ashes

Tai Ikomi

His Beauty For My Ashes

Printed in the United States of America

MORRIS PUBLISHING

3212 East Highway 30 • Kearney, NE 68847 • 1-800-650-7888

Unless otherwise indicated, Scriptures are taken from the King James Version of the Bible.

ISBN 1-890430-91-9

Published By
Triumph Publishing
P. O. Box 690158
Bronx, New York, 10469

Dedication

This book is dedicate to the loving memory of Johnny, my late husband and our precious little ones, Temple, Tai and Kennie.

Thank you for the joy you gave to me through your lives

TABLE OF CONTENT

Chapter

Foreword

The redeeming power of Jesus Christ to turn a tragedy into victory is certainly expressed in this book.

If anyone ever had a reason to harbor a grudge or to be bitter, Taiwo has. But through the blood of Jesus Christ, and the power of the Holy Spirit she conquered her emotions. The forward look to a reunion with her precious family is a joy to read about.

One has to believe in a Heaven and a good God after reading this beautiful story.

Having gone through some of the same emotions that Taiwo experienced, because of the death of my daughter and son, I was moved with compassion by her story. But I also experienced with her the same exhilaration in my spirit as he allowed God to heal her wounds.

Anyone who has gone through a tragedy and is having a struggle because of it should read this book

Evelyn (Oral) Roberts

Preface

The story of how I lost my entire family is not an easy one to write. My natural tendency is to push this task as far from me as possible.

However, on the spiritual plane, a surge of divine strength seems to fill my inner core. This strength is the anchor behind the writing of this book.

Fellow Christians have urged me to pen the story of my tragedy in order to minister to the bereaved, who can be difficult to reach. Therefore, for their sakes, and even more to the glory of God, I must write.

Yet I recognized that I could not undertake such an endeavor without the prompting of the Holy Spirit. There must be a divine timing. For this timing I have waited patiently, careful not to rush and yet not to lag behind.

The divine moment, I believe, has come. The time to lay bare my soul is now. It is my faith in the Lord Jesus Christ, that His grace will guide my pen to reach the heart. Bereavement is hard to accept. Only God can reach the heart and whisper His peace and assurance.

The Lord is by no means responsible for the mishaps that have befallen the human race, but He is able to turn those situations around. Jesus Christ is still on the Throne. He is still sovereign. In this knowledge and assurance I take my repose.

Part One

The Tragedy

Chapter

1

Journey To Fayetteville.

Easter Sunday, March 30, 1986...a glorious time for our family as we celebrated the Resurrection. Little did I know it was the last Sunday I would spend with my precious loved ones. Only a week earlier Johnny, my husband, had agonized in the spirit of prayer. He had sensed death hovering over someone in the prayer meeting we had attended never realizing he was the one who was to die.

Weeks prior to this, he had repeatedly told me that something good was going to happen to him soon. It was a strong feeling in his spirit. We never dreamed it was to be his time to go home to be with the Lord. The apostle Paul wrote to the Philippians, "for to me to live is Christ, and to die is gain" Philippians. 1:21. Johnny was having this foretaste of heaven.

The Easter Sunday morning had been refreshing and Johnny was excited about it. The pastor had talked about the resurrection of Christ and its implications. We, as Christians, Pastor Rodney Hinrichs pointed out, have this blessed hope of resurrection. As we drove home, Johnny asked me what I thought of the sermon. Excitement was written on his face and I saw that he had been deeply touched in an unusual way. All I could say was that I had been blessed too. Looking back now, I do not recollect specifically what Johnny said; but I wonder if the Lord was imparting the consciousness to him that his own resurrection was near.

We arrived home, and after lunch went to the sitting room. Suddenly, I felt depression in my spirit but could not understand why. I thought maybe I had missed God in some way, so I excused myself and went to the bedroom to pray. I was determined not to get up until I heard from the Lord. A depressive spirit was simply not part of my life style.

After five or ten minutes, the Lord told me I would be going to Nigeria that summer. It sounded incredible. How could we go when we did not have enough money for Johnny's college tuition? Nevertheless, I got up, satisfied that I could still hear from the Lord. In a time like this, I especially needed to pray and tarry for the power of the Holy Spirit in my life as I was used to doing. But how could I, when other things were clamoring for my attention? I was a full-time housewife and a mother of three. I remember telling my husband afterward that I wished I were a male pastor so I could devote much more time to prayer. He smiled.

An hour later, I was mentally going through my schedule for the week. I had an appointment for my twin children on the first of April, which fell on the next Tuesday. But I felt in my spirit that I was not to going to keep it. I had wondered why. I didn't know that by then the twins would not be alive.

At 7 p.m., my husband made an impromptu decision. He wanted to visit the University of Arkansas at Fayetteville, where he had applied to do his graduate studies. The original plan was that we would all go to Fayetteville to get an idea of what the place was like before we moved there. But, because of this short notice, he was going to take along only our eldest son, Temple, who was very enthusiastic about the journey.

I readily agreed with the plan. With them out of the way I would be able to catch up with my household chores. Six weeks earlier, Johnny had lost his job, and his presence at home had made it virtually impossible for me to cover my daily assignments. He wanted my attention all the time. He would ask me to leave my household chores and talk with him. Making time for one another would soon prove to be the fitting climax of our marriage.

They were to head for Fayetteville that same evening. Suddenly, Johnny asked me to come along with him for companionship. I declined. He persisted and I promised I would pray over it.

I had to pray about it because the Lord had told me sometime before that I was to go to Fayetteville only once. I had taken it to mean that I was not meant to go until the final time. Of course, I did not know that there wouldn't be a second time?

If I readily agreed to go with him, I might find myself disobeying a direct order from the Lord. Besides, Johnny and I respected each other's spiritual convictions. So it was not unusual for me to tell him I was going to pray about it, and more so in light of the circumstances.

Then I heard the voice of the Lord say, "Go with him." That was good enough for me. When I told Johnny the Lord said I should go with him, what joy appeared on his face! We were all going on this journey after all.

At 11 p.m. we were ready to go. The two-and-a-half-year-old twins, our daughter Ejima and our son Tosan, were harnessed to their seats. Temple, who was eight, sat in between them.

It was time to pray and commit the journey to the Lord. I felt something strange in my spirit. It was as if someone had poured an ocean into my heart. I had never sensed this before. It was not like previous times when an uneasiness in my spirit was indicative of an impending danger.

I prayed. Then Johnny prayed. I asked him if he felt what I felt. Yes, he too had a strange feeling in his spirit. Neither of us felt we should not go, and so, committing the trip unto the Lord, we set out on this fateful journey.

We arrived in Fayetteville the following day. Johnny left us in a park close to the university while he took care of his mission. The rest of us had fun that evening. It was Temple's birthday. How could I have know it was our last day together We played and laughed; we took turns chasing and catching one another.

Johnny returned, and soon we were on our way back to Lincoln, Nebraska. When we were out on the open highway I convinced Johnny to allow me to drive. I got behind the steering wheel. About fifteen minutes later, the Lord forbade me to continue to drive. I told Johnny, who understood, and he took over once again. After half an hour or so, he said he was feeling sleepy so we took the next exit. We slept in the car outside a hotel as we did not have enough cash on us to rent a room. At about 1 a.m. we continued our journey.

Chapter

2

THE ACCIDENT

April 1, 1986...may I never again experience such a day! My husband was driving, and I was awake to keep him company. The children were asleep. It was a little after 1 a.m and it was raining. I looked at my husband and my love for him filled my heart. It was like falling in love for the first time with this man I had married nine years earlier.

I was baffled, by the sudden rush of emotion. Undoubtedly, he had been good to me and I had learned to enjoy his moral support. Only a few hours earlier, on our way to Fayetteville, I had expressed my gratitude to God and also to my husband that I had married him. I told him that I felt secure and protected under his strength.

I had implicit trust in his ability as the head of our

home and I knew he was always there for me. Johnny was a wise and hardworking man; next to God, he was the one I trusted most.

I could not explain the feeling I had in my heart. "Darling" I blurted out "I think I am falling in love with you again." His eyes lit up. A smile spread across his face.

Can I ever forget the glitter and love in those eyes? It was as though he were already at the heavenly portals; the next fifteen minutes would find him there with the children. He placed his hand on my leg and gave it a gentle squeeze. I felt so proud that I was the recipient of such love and security from such a wonderful man! I truly believe that Johnny went to his eternal home full of love for his God and for his wife.

We approached a construction zone on Highway in Plattecity, Missouri. I pointed out the signs and suggested he slow, down which he did. A lighted arrow was directing the two-lane traffic to one lane. Suddenly, I heard a bang, then felt the impact of being struck from behind. Although I did not realize what had happened, the noise of it sent an unending echo to my ears.

The next thing I remembered hearing two men knocking on the car window on my side. Not knowing where I was, or what had happened, I instinctively rolled it down. The men must have asked me to get out of the car, for I reached for the seat belt.

That was the last I remembered and the last I saw of those two men. I was later to recognize that they were angels sent to rescue me. It seems a long time ago now, but the appearance of those angels is still fresh in my memory.

I learned later that the first man to arrive at the scene of the accident did not see the angels. Instead, he saw me climbing out of a ditch and thought I was an alien from outer space! To this day, I am still unable to recollect how I ended up in the ditch.

I realized a miracle had happened, one that I was not even aware of; God had sent two angels to rescue me from the fiery accident. The coroner later said that he had "no earthly idea" of how I managed to be outside of the car.

My lawyer said the police department has not been able to figure out how I got out. It was a miracle of the Almighty.

When I came to, I found myself outside of the car. Many people were present. I looked back and saw that the rear of the car was on fire. I realized immediately that my family was in that fire. I dashed towards the car, but I was helpless since the doors were jammed. My mental faculties were not coordinating.

Some men at the scene were doing their best to put out the fire. One man yelled for a fire extinguisher. Another man ran to his trailer to get one, but it was too late. Oh, the agony of that moment! My family was dying and I could do nothing to save them.

Suddenly I heard the cry of my two-and-a-half-year-old daughter in the car. I went to the other side of the car to get her out, but I was unable to get in. Fear gripped me. I knew instantly that cry would haunt me in my dreams for the rest of my life. I could not leave the scene. I had to stay there and hope that somehow I would be able to save her.

I did not know God was going to turn that same cry into a sweet memory of the last cry I heard from my daughter, teaching me that with God all things are possible. She became quiet after three or four outbursts. All became still. I sensed she was struggling, fighting for her life. All continued to be quiet in the car. Peace and tranquility seemed to descend upon it. In retrospect, I remember the scripture which says, "The death of his saints is precious in his sight." The Lord Jesus Christ was there.

The fire continued to blaze as it spread through the rest of the car. It became obvious that there was nothing more anybody could do. The men who were there moved back to watch the end. I could not. I ran from the scene crying and throwing my hands into the air. The sight of them in the flames was more than I could bear. Unable to contain the shock, I began to call on God.

Then, a man approached me and led me to his truck. I followed him, not caring where I was going or what would become of me. He asked me to lie on my stomach on the floor of a truck. I suddenly became aware of the excruciating pain in my back. Soon the man left and I lay there.

Outside was my family, trapped in an uncontrollable fire, while inside I lay bound by excruciating pain. My brain could not seem to hold the two sufferings. All I could think of was my back and my pain. I wanted to think of my family, but the pain in my back would not allow it.

The man came back. He told me the ambulance was on its way. After thanking him, I complained of the pain and asked if I could get up to ease it. He advised me not to, since too much movement could do irreparable damage to my back, which could lead to paralysis. Once again fear gripped me. Has the damage been done? Am I going to face a life of paralysis? The thought of it was unbearable.

It seemed as though an eternity had passed when the ambulance finally arrived. I was carefully laid on a stretcher and placed inside. Soon we were on our way to the hospital. After answering the preliminary questions in the emergency room, I was sent to X-ray.

If I thought the pain in my back was unbearable while I lay inside the van, I was wrong. The pain doubled as I was shifted from one side to the other for the X-rays. When the X-rays were finally over, I was taken to another room.

My eyes were closed when I sensed someone close to me. I opened my eyes to find a police officer. He was stooping by my bed with one knee on the floor and, as gently as he could, he told me what had happened. A nineteen-year-old boy had struck our car from the rear. The impact of his high speed had sparked the fire that snuffed out the life of my family.

There was no reaction on my part. I was too tired physically and emotionally to give away the little energy that I had. I remember being struck by the kindness of this officer, though. I thanked him for the information.

He then asked for my next of kin. I wanted to give him the telephone number of my pastor, but my mind went blank. Instead, I gave him an educated guess of a close friend's number. After further medical questions, I was wheeled to my room.

The reality of the accident continued to evade me. A few hours passed, and the door opened. It was my pastor. He had received news about the accident and had travelled the 150 miles to see me. He did not say a word, but came straight to me and gave me a strong squeeze. His silence was more effective than any words he could have uttered. His eyes were penetrating as he tried to determine the effect of the tragedy on me.

I began to talk for I wanted to exonerate myself. I had blamed myself for not being able to save my family. If only I had dragged Johnny along after unbuckling myself, even though I was not conscious of my circumstances. After recounting the incident, I stopped. There was a silence. Then I began to wave a good-bye to my departed husband: " Good-bye, Johnny Good-bye."

The phone rang. It was the Lincoln Starr. They wanted an interview with me, but I did not want to answer any questions. I remember being surprised that news had reached the press. My pastor picked up the phone, and I motioned to him to answer their questions.

At 3 p.m., my pastor was ready to drive back to Lincoln. He promised he would be back the following day to see me. However, I felt it was too much for him to travel the distance again. So I asked my doctor if I could be released. He gave me a clean bill of health and released me after making me promise to report to my doctor upon my arrival at Lincoln. The X-rays had showed no broken bones in my body and he believed I could undertake the journey. Soon we were on our way back home

Chapter

3

Back Home To Lincoln

When I arrived at the pastor's house, his wife Marilyn was there to welcome me and to make me comfortable. I was made to feel at home - something I needed at the time. News of the accident had spread far and wide, as it had been announced over the radio as well as on television. From then on, my pastor was to be my spokesman for the press. All I was to learn about further developments concerning the accident I learned from the media.

Friends came to visit me and try to comfort me in my sorrow, but what could they say that would reach my distraught soul? I knew I had to hear from God. Why did my entire family have to die? Why die we not see the impending danger? The questions were not to challenge God, but to get answers.

In the past, the Lord had often alerted my husband and me of any impending dangers. But what were they compared with this tragedy? I knew God had to give me an answer. My mind could find no rest until I heard from above.

Wednesday, April 2...I continued to wait for the answer from God. Finally, at 7p.m. I heard the words, "Go and Pray". The Lord had spoken. With mixed feelings I quickly excused myself from a sister who had come to visit me and headed for my room. I had hardly begun to pray when the Lord gave me a vision.

I saw a wall stretched as far as my eyes could see; in the middle of the wall was a hole that gave me a glimpse of what was behind it. There was a light, and how sharp and bright it was! The next moment, I heard the Lord say that my loved ones were encircled in that light. He then proceeded to tell why the reason for the accident.

I got up, relieved that God was still in charge. He was still the God of all flesh and He was still directing the affairs of men. My husband and the children were in a far better place. They had become citizens of heaven where Christ is the light that brightens the very atmosphere. They had passed through fire which lasted only a moment compared to the eternity of bliss which had now become theirs. They had passed from death unto life.

Oh, how I appreciated the death of Jesus Christ in that moment! He had shed His blood to pave the way to heaven for those who would believe. Heaven became a breath away from me because my family was there. I began to appreciate more and more the blessed hope Christians have, all because our Lord Jesus saw our helpless state and came to offer this wonderful salvation.

Yes, the Son of God became the Son of man that men might become the sons of God. The Son of God left heaven for earth that men might leave earth and go to heaven. The Son of God suffered, bled, and died that men might live.

What a wonderful Savior! What a wonderful Lord!

Friday, April 4...my first visit to our apartment since the accident. A Christian brother accompanied me.

I was naturally filled with apprehension, unsure of the effect on me emotionally. As I opened the door, all was still. There was no voice to welcome me home. My family was truly gone. It had only been four days earlier that we were all there. We had all set out on that fatal journey, but they did not return to see the house they left behind.

Tears ran down my cheeks. But the full impact of their permanent departure was still absent. I looked around briefly and left. It was no joy to remain there.

The following day, the pastor suggested I should go to our apartment alone. I agreed. I went straight into the children's room. As I stood there, recollections of them started pouring in. Suddenly I heard a voice. It was not audible, but it was crystal clear. The exact words were, "They still love you." What joy filled my heart knowing that they still remembered and loved me.

No doubt they were waiting for the moment when I would draw my last breath and hasten my steps to the heavenly portals where they would welcome me to my eternal home. Then we would meet again, this time never to part. What a day of unalloyed joy that will be!

On Thursday, news of the accident had reached my family back home. Someone had called a friend of ours in Nigeria who broke the news to our families. Both families went into shock, I was later told. It was decided that the funeral should take place here. My mother and my twin sister would come to the United States. Johnny's cousin and former sponsor from Ohio would also come for the funeral.

My mother and twin sister were due to arrive on Sunday, April 6th, as they could not get their visas in time. Their flight was to arrive in Omaha, about an hour's drive from Lincoln.

The pastor and his wife drove me. On the way, the Lord told me that He wanted to speak to me. Before this time, I had decided not to file a lawsuit against the boy who had hit us, a decision based on the Word of God concerning forgiveness. Now, the Lord spoke to me and expressly commanded me not to sue him. That brought the issue to a complete rest.

When we arrived at the airport my mother and my twin sister were waiting for us. And with mixed emotions we hugged each other. Soon we were on our way back to Lincoln. That same day, my mother and sister and I moved back to my apartment.

Chapter

4

The Funeral

The day of the funeral finally came. It was Tuesday the eighth of April..another day that was to remain indelible in my memory.

The memory of the accident flashed through my mind. I was numb. I was not exactly sure how to welcome this event that must unfold before the end of the day. It was now a week since the terrible accident had claimed the lives of my husband and our three precious children. The agony of watching them die was almost unbearable.

Today, I was going go bury my loved ones. Indeed, this same day I had to watch their casket being lowered into the grave. Eight days before, they were with me; but they were no longer here. They had gone to the other world, beyond my touch, beyond my sight, beyond my reach; but not beyond my love. Oh, the agony of that moment!

Why, oh why did they have to die?

I remained calm. I knelt by my bed and praised God for the day. Next, I went to see my sister in another room. She suggested we sing aloud the praises of God. For a moment I hesitated. How could I raise my voice and sing on such a day as this - the day I was going to bury my family? I was not too sure such singing was appropriate for the day.

Nevertheless, I decided to go ahead with her suggestion. We were on the second or third song when something happened inside of me. For the first time since their departure, I felt united with my departed loved ones. It was a feeling of closeness that is difficult to define or express.

My family was singing God's praises in heaven, while I was engaged in the same worship down below. We had the same Object of praise. We were praising the same Creator. Distance was no barrier as our hearts melted into one in gratitude to the One who has made us partakers of eternal life. At that moment I experienced the power inherent in praising the Almighty God!

The hours rolled by quickly. At 2:30 p.m. we set out for the cemetery. The casket was hung just above the ground. It was closed. I had requested that it be that way, as their remains were no longer intact. I had also wished that they should be buried together. They had died together, and I believed that on Resurrection Day they would be raised together.

I was not desirous of seeing their ravaged remains. I preferred to see them, in my mind, as vibrant, healthy and happy. And to this day I have not regretted the decision.

I got out of the car, and I went straight to their casket. Tears began pouring from my eyes. The reality of their deaths was still not there. My head had assented to their death but my heart would not let go. As my fingers ran across their names, which had been engraved on the coffin, thoughts started pouring into my mind. Is this the end? Are you really in there? Are we never again to be together on this earth? At this point, I was ushered to my seat for the commencement of the service.

The pastor opened the service with a Bible reading and a short commentary, as he reiterated his hope of the resurrection. Next came the song which I had chosen because it was our family's favorite song.

Redeemed - how I love to proclaim it!

Redeemed by the blood of the Lamb;

Redeemed through His infinite mercy

His child, and forever, I am.

Redeemed, Redeemed,

Redeemed by the blood of the Lamb;

Redeemed, Redeemed,

His child, and forever, I am.

The song hit me like an electrical wave. My soul suddenly became rapturous. I became a changed person instantly, though I could not understand the transaction.

I found myself amidst the angelic host in the spiritual realm. The atmosphere seemed to be filled with such a great brightness that it did not seem possible. I felt the atmosphere lit by praises, not only of the heavenly host, which included my family, but all of nature seemed to burst out literally in worship to the Almighty.

All I wanted to do was join the heavenly host and my beloved ones beyond in spirit in praising our dear Redeemer. And that was exactly what I did. With my hands lifted up and my heart burning with praise, I offered glory and honor with my lips to the One who had given me hope of eternal life with Jesus Christ, the Son of the living God. Before startled and amazed visitors, I praised God with a voice vibrant with emotion. Instead of a funeral service, the Holy Spirit, the One in charge, turned it into a praise service.

It was an experience that has stayed with me. I am most indebted to the Lord of Glory who compassed me with such strength. Now I can truly say "Thank You, Jesus, for taking care of me and of my family yonder. I have no adequate means of praising You, but this one life that I have shall be spent in Your service.

In Your mercy and faithfulness, show me the path that leads to Your perfect will and I will walk in it. With my whole being and all that I have, will I praise You and exalt Your wonderful name"

In the evening, a second funeral service was held, this time in our church, Rejoice in the Lord Lutheran Church. I planned to dress in white because I wanted to join my family in wearing that color. The Holy spirit had earlier changed the funeral service from a time of mourning into a time of rejoicing. Why should I change the mood?

The funeral service went well. I had told my pastor that the focus of his sermon should be on Christ and the salvation He has to offer. Hopefully, someone in the audience would accept His salvation. He agreed and the hope of eternal life was the theme of his sermon.

What assurance we have in Christ! My consolation resided in the hope of eternal life with Jesus. Thank God, Johnny was a Christian here on earth. He had surrendered his life to Christ and lived for Him, and now he had become a permanent resident of heaven!

Temple, our eldest son, had accepted Christ into his heart when he was four and a half. He was so young then, but he had expressed his desire to give his life to Jesus. Together, Johnny and I had led him to Christ. He was confident Christ had honored his request and had come into his heart.

The following morning, he looked at his stomach, then at us and said "Mummy, Daddy, my tummy is so big because Jesus came into my heart yesterday." Johnny explained that Jesus came into his heart and not his stomach. We all laughed about it.

Temple was an avid reader. He read anything he could lay his hands on. I had bought a lot of books but had discouraged him from reading the Bible, as I did not want him to develop any negative attitude toward the Bible which might be difficult to change later. Instead, I inundated him with children's Bible stories. However, six weeks before the accident Johnny helped me to get over my fear and allowed him to read the Bible.

It was like throwing meat to a hungry lion. From then on, Temple buried himself in the Bible. Anywhere he went, he took it with him. Even on the day we travelled, he carried it. By this time he was halfway through the Bible. A few days after he had gone to be with the Lord, the Lord told me He was preparing Temple for heaven through the Word.

Now, his eyes can behold what he had been reading. All the questions he was asking his father and me he can now direct to the One who has perfect knowledge of all things. What a wonderful moment for my son!

The twins were not old enough to understand or experience the new birth. They did, however, know the name of Jesus. I used to teach them numbers using the name of Jesus, which they repeated after me. For example, I would say "One, Jesus is Lord. Two, Jesus is Christ. Three, Praise the Lord." Little did I realize how close they were to seeing the same Lord face to face and praising Him.

Part Two

After The Tragedy

Chapter

5

The Aftermath

By the following week the reality of my hus band and children's deaths was now begin ning to dawn on me. My heart was sorely wounded. Thank God, Christians all over the world were praying for me. I was stable most of the time, but once in a while sorrow like sea billows would engulf me. However, I knew where to turn - to the secret place of the Most High.

In those early days following the accident, I did not pray very much, compared with the two to three hours that had been my custom. I believe that those hours of prayer must have helped prepare me for this loss. Whenever my heart started to ache and become weighed down with a tremendous burden that no words can describe, I would rush away to pray.

Hardly two minutes would pass when the sorrow would be lifted and I would be strong again. It was like filling my car's tank with fuel. When my strength waned, I went for a fill-up where the supply never runs dry. I received strength in exchange for my weakness.

In fact, there came a time when I actually rejoiced that they had left this earthly city for the heavenly abode. Yes, I did miss them; but what joy had become theirs now. And for their sakes I joined them in their joy.

When I knelt to pray, the Lord would speak to me. One day, I was contemplating our last day in the park and I remembered the fun we were all having when suddenly broke into my thoughts. He said that the fun they had that in the park was like a dirty rag compared to what is theirs now.

The Lord continued to shower His love on me. There was hardly any request I made of the Lord that I did not receive. Often, I would ask Him to speak to me and He would. Oftentimes, when I did not expect to hear from him , His voice would come, clear as crystal. He told me a lot about myself, my future ministry, and my family beyond.

I would wonder at myself and the inner strength I was exhibiting. I thought that I was losing my mind for not wallowing in depression and self pity. At other times,

I would simply acknowledge that I was a recipient of the grace that can only come from above.

The gentleness of the Spirit was delightful during this period. I understood the verse that says *"A bruised reed shall he not break."* (Isaiah 42:3) The Spirit was my best Friend and my comforter in my desolation and loss. No human words could penetrate my distraught soul to remove the hurt. My refuge was with the Lord. And to Him I must turn.

In my own little way, I can now understand how our Lord received strength in the Garden of Gethsemane to endure His crucifixion. In a matter of hours He was going to carry the sins of the world. He knew its inevitable result - a brief separation from God. He prayed for strength. His Father was there to strengthen Him. And throughout the trial and the crucifixion He remained unruffled and perfectly fearless.

Dear friend no matter what may be the circumstances surrounding of your life, there is a God in heaven who can see you through. His is the last word. No one can override His decree. He says "I work, who can hinder it?" He can make a way where you deem impossible. He will give you that inner strength that will help you to live above your circumstances. I have been there and I can testify that indeed, with God all things are possible.

I heard the invitation of the Lord Jesus Christ "Come unto me, all ye that labor and are heavy laden and I will give you rest." (Matthew 11:28) I turned to Him in my distress and He filled my life with peace that defies human analysis. He taught me that there is absolutely nothing beyond His power or His reach.

One of the most baffling experiences I had was related to the cry of my daughter in the car. I had thought that cry would haunt me. No, the Lord did not wipe the memory from my mind. What He did, to my amazement, was to replace the bad memory with one that was sweet. It was sweet in the sense that I had the privilege of hearing her lovely sweet voice once again, uttered though it may have been under a bad circumstance.

What a miracle! Wonder of wonders! What can God not accomplish? He is the God of unlimited resources. Direct your gaze to the Living God as revealed in Jesus Christ. Only then can you live above your circumstances!

Grief, not depression, filled my heart. There is a difference between the two. Depression is staying unduly long in grief. The period of grief has helped me to unburden myself. The focus of my grief was on Johnny, my husband, since he was the one I missed the most. However after crying I would have a sense of relief. I cannot recount how many times I grieved over him.

In those days I loved looking at my family's photographs as a source of to comfort me. One day, I brought out the pictures to look at them as usual. When I saw

Johnny's photograph, I was comforted. Next came the children's. There was no reaction or emotional response from me.

I sensed something was amiss. Then it dawned on me that I had not really grieved for them as I had for Johnny. I loved them, but my attention had been on Johnny. I realized later that my heart could only grieve for one person at a time. Such was the magnitude of my loss.

With this realization, I decided to grieve for my three little children. I would take each of their photographs one by one and I would cry over it. In this way, I was able to let out my grief. Soon I was able to look at their pictures with mixed emotions, joy about their present state, and sadness because we were no longer together.

Chapter

6

The Journey to Nigeria

In May, I was admitted to the University of Nebraska to take my master's degree in French. School was not to begin until the end of August, so I had a few weeks to spend in Nigeria. Before my embarking on this journey, the Lord told me I was to spend much time in Bible reading.

When I arrived in Nigeria, my family and friends were waiting at the airport, eager to embrace me and to welcome me home. It was a touching scene as we embraced one another after such a long absence. It had been eight years since I left them for Britain.

While I waited for my luggage, my mind flashed back to the story of Naomi. How similar were our circumstances! Naomi had left her country with her husband and their two sons. But she returned with none of them, for they had all died in the foreign land. I had left Nigeria in May, 1977, to join my fiance Johnny in England, and I had returned to Nigeria with neither my husband nor my children.

Johnny and I attended the same fellowship and we were sure we were meant for each other, for our union seemed ordained. A Christian brother had given me a description of the man I was going to marry, even though neither of us had yet met Johnny. A friend of Johnny's, who was a perfect stranger to me, had also given Johnny a description of the girl he was meant to marry.

In a vision Johnny had also seen me praying and the Lord told him I was to be his wife. It was a Scripture that confirmed this union in my case. We became engaged a few months after he proposed to me. Johnny went to Britain to further his studies and I was to meet him there where we would marry.

We were married on the second of July, 1977, in Grimsby, England. It was a beautiful day and the future looked bright. Nine months later, on the 31st of March, our first son, Temple Onaoritshebawo, was born. I had become a mother and Johnny a father! Oh, what joy filled our soul!

Five years later, we moved to the United States of America, where Johnny continued with his studies in food science and technology. In 1983, the twins were born. Our daughter Ejima Taiwo came first. Thirty-five minutes later, her twin brother Tosanwumi Kehinde also arrived. I had always wanted twins, as I am one. To crown the joy, they were born on my mother's birthday, the 20th of September! Temple, then five and a half, considered himself the most fortunate brother in the world for having a brother and a sister born at the same time. Johnny and I tried to bring the children up in the ways of the Lord.

Yet, here was I, coming back to Nigeria with nothing to show for all those years. I came back the same way I had gone. Yet, I knew God was with me and He would make His plan known in due course.

I began to divide my time between the Bible and my French review. I did not realize I was going out of God's will, disobeying the heavenly injunction. Instead of burying myself in the Word, as God had commanded me earlier, I divided the time with the French review. This disobedience was accompanied by a deep depression, so acute I could barely be still.

It was the first time I sank into depression. All around was bright, but inside was darkness. I thus found myself in a tunnel, out of the reach of any human being. No one could walk the road with me, so narrow it was. My family did the best they could, giving me that sense of belonging which can only come from one's family. My mother treated me like an egg that must not be dropped. She would try to comfort me, but her words could not reach me.

For the first time, I got angry with God. I challenged Him for asking me to join Johnny in that fateful journey. I reasoned that, if I had followed my "better judgment," at least I would still have the twins. You see, I was operating out of God's grace. And without His grace, I would think and act just as an ordinary human being. But there was no need for me to be in this depressive mood. No, not with the grace of the Lord Jesus Christ that was within my reach.

Then I did something foolish. I told God, "You killed my twin children." Immediately, I realized I had sinned against the Lord who had been so good to me. There and then, I asked forgiveness from the Lord. Still there was no change in my circumstance. Finally, I saw the reason for my acute depression. I stopped reviewing my French.

Then I asked the Lord to show me my family in their glorified state. I told my sister to agree with me, for I am a great believer in the prayer of agreement, and she did. I expected the vision within the next week. But the Lord gave me the vision the following day. This was typical of the Lord's dealings with me in those days. Almost all my requests were granted beyond my expectations.

The following night, as we all sang God's praises,

I saw a vision. I saw Johnny seated on something I could not see. He was playing a musical instrument. Behind him was a huge man, standing as if he were his companion. Johnny's eyes were radiating with an inexpressible joy. The color of his garment was white, yet it was translucent. What a glorious appearance he had!

When I saw this vision, I thought I was imagining it. The vision disappeared. Then the Spirit of God came on me in a liquid form. I heard the words, "You are not imagining it, you are being privileged to see into the spiritual realm." Immediately, the vision came back.

This time I was convinced that I had received a divine visitation. The vision swept away my depression as joy once again flooded my soul. I continued this way for many weeks to come.

The Bible says the mercies of the Lord are new every morning {Lamentations. 3:22-23}. His goodness to me is overwhelming. If His compassion is over all that He has made, as Psalm 148:8 declares, how much more compassion will He show to us, His children? Why, it will be fathomless!

A month passed. It was now July; the time to leave Nigeria was drawing near. I had to return to the United States to begin my classes. I was rather apprehensive about my French studies, as I had prepared only a little. But I had to trust that everything was under control. I did not realize that the Lord had other plans in mind.

One day, as I got up from my bed, I heard the Lord tell me I was to go to a Bible school. I did not like the idea. However, I had learned that if I want to walk with the Lord, I must do so on His terms. I told Him that where He led I would follow. I trusted in His wisdom knowing that the thoughts He had for me are thoughts of good and not of evil. The Lord then told me that He would confirm it through a brother I was to see that evening, and I was satisfied.

I kept my appointment to see the brother that evening. In the course of the visit, I told him of my plans to attend a Bible school. I thought it wise not to mention that he was meant to confirm this decision. Every prophecy, if it is of God, should be able to stand the scrutiny of examination.

His first reaction was to discourage me. I was puzzled by this. Then it was time to pray. He laid hands on me, but he could not pray. Instead, he began to prophesy that I was to go to Bible school, for it was the Lord's will. As soon as he said those words, I felt comfort in a liquid form go through my nerves. I could hardly hold such unspeakable joy, yet I was enjoying it. For the very first time since the accident, I realized I was truly being comforted. Previously I had experienced healing in various forms. However, this time I was profoundly comforted. This stream of comfort was to continue flowing through my veins for a day or two.

The Scriptures speak of the comfort of the Holy

Spirit. Jesus called Him the Comforter, who alone can comfort those who mourn. This is the type of comfort that is effective. The Word of God energized by the Holy Spirit, can reach the recesses of the heart with comfort. Since God is omnipresent, there is no place hidden from Him. Distance cannot stand in the way of His miracles. Whatever the situation in which you may find yourself, the Savior knows no barriers or impossibilities.

If you will simply acknowledge Him as Lord, you will experience the comfort of the Holy Spirit. *"The Spirit of the Lord God is upon me...to comfort all that mourn; to appoint unto them that mourn in Zion, to give unto them beauty for ashes, the oil of joy for mourning, the garment of praise for the spirit of heaviness..."* [Isaiah 61: 1-3] This is my testimony.

At the end of July, I went back to the United States with my twin sister to attend the Kenneth Hagin camp meeting. It was a time of refreshing. After the camp meeting I went back to Lincoln, Nebraska. Until this time, I still did not know which Bible school to attend. I had asked the Lord to tell me, but He didn't. Instead I was to wait and allow God to unfold His plans in His own time.

This was a new dimension for me. I was used to knowing what the future held, for the Lord often revealed it to me if I asked Him. It was not an easy experience, but the Lord was the Master, and I, the follower.

Two weeks passed. I had applied to Christ For The Nations in Dallas Texas, but I had not received any reply from the school. One Sunday morning, while I was still in bed, I heard the voice of the Lord tell me that Christ For The Nations was His choice for me. I began to pack. The following day, I called the school and was told that I still needed some things before my admission was finalized. I told them I was on my way to Dallas with the rest of the requirements. They had no objection, and so I found myself in the plane the following day, headed for Dallas.

My stay at Christ For The Nations was fruitful, both academically and spiritually. I was required to live in the dormitory. The spiritual climate was conducive to my inner healing. A community of Christians where Christ is the center of its activities was what I needed, and the courses were excellent. Thus, I had the best of two worlds.

Part Three

Victory Over The Tragedy

Chapter

7

The Grace of God

I need to say something about my walk with God. Gone were the days when I could get by with twenty to thirty minute devotions. I had to go back to the schedule I followed before the accident. I spent an average of four hours a day with the Lord. This was in obedience to the command of the Lord that I was to spend an hour with Him, in the morning, one in the afternoon, and one in the evening.

I can distinctly remember one afternoon as I knelt praying; I felt the presence of the Lord to my right in a powerful. I became still, knowing He wanted to speak. It was a note of warning. The Lord cautioned me not to default in my prayer lest the devil find a loophole in my life, I took the warning seriously. I followed the admonition rigidly. From then on, whether I liked it or not, I knew I must pray at least three hours a day.

I found a resting place in those hours of prayer, for by now the grim reality of the accident was weighing heavily on me. It was a place I could bring my weakness in exchange for His strength. Soon, I began to look forward to these times of prayer. I had to fill my life constantly with the presence of the Lord. Who else could fill the place my family held in my affection? Others may be able to afford not to pray but I could not, for sorrow would overcome me. This was what was keeping me from falling apart.

Yet in the midst of it all, I felt fulfilled. I was elated in my spirit. I could not understand it though. It was simply the grace of God that was working in me. I was experiencing the supporting presence of the Lord which Paul also knew when the Lord told him that His grace was sufficient for him. It had been sufficient for Paul. It was also sufficient for me.

Paul lay in prison awaiting a possible death sentence. Yet, he could write to the Philippians that for him to live was Christ and to die was gain. Death held no terror to him for within was the Prince of Life, the One who died that he might live. This inner peace in the face of all odds is the heritage of Christians. Paul knew the power of this grace. No wonder he began nearly all his letters by proclaiming this wonderful grace!

Praise God this grace is never depleted. It runs from the highest mountain to the lowest valley. And praise God, this grace has not lost its ancient touch.

Friends often thought that I was exhibiting my strong points and hiding my moments of despair. They simply could not understand the joy that radiated through my life. One Christian friend even went so far as to suggest that I should challenge God and be angry with Him in order to let out my anger. Of course, he meant well, but I told him that I could not, for I knew that He is a good God. The grace of God was strengthening my inner being. Try as I might to find fault with God, I could not, simply because I knew God was a benevolent God.

His very essence is love, as 1John 4:8 tells us. No, the fault was not with God. He had saved me from my sins and brought me into His fold when I was a rebel and alien to His Kingdom. The Bible says that when we were yet sinners Christ died for us. He gave us His only begotten Son to die for the sins of man.

How could the God who gave me His very best turn around and do me such harm or even allow it for no reason? Such were my thoughts. I could not blaspheme God. I could not sin against His Holy Name. What was the reason for this rationalization? I believe it was the grace of God. Hebrews 4:16 encourages us to go to the throne of God, where grace abounds: "Let us therefore come boldly unto the throne of grace, that we may obtain mercy, and find grace to help in time of need." I followed the prescription and went to the throne of grace through spending time with God, and I received help in time of my need.

The same grace also saw me though my grieving period. Despite this tremendous loss, I was not despondent, nor did I feel I was at the end of life's rope. My heart was filled with a strange serenity amidst the turbulence. Joy often filled my soul, not only at the thought of my family's present state, but also at the thought that God was still on the throne. The joy of the Lord thus became the source of my strength.

Once in a while, when grief would overwhelm me, I would go and pray, crying before the Lord as I poured out my heart to Him. Almost immediately, joy and peace would become mine again. This approach was more common during the early phase of my grief. However, six months later, when the Lord told me to spend at least three hours a day with Him, I found that I was rarely overwhelmed with grief.

Time spent in His presence became the antidote for prolonged and frequent grieving moments. The reality of the loss was present, but so was the grace of God.

I thank God for this grace, which is beyond the sphere of human understanding. My human imagination could not have grasped the greatness of its power, except as I experienced it through my loss. Alongside my grief was the grace of Jesus Christ that wiped away the tears that poured from my eyes. Grief was necessary in time of loss so that healing could take place. But the grace of God did not allow this grief to overcome me and make my life a misery as long as I walked in His will.

What more can I say about this wonderful grace — the wonder of our salvation, the bedrock of our Christian existence? It has not lost its ancient power. The hardest sinners have experienced this grace that can blot out sins of the blackest type. They heard of this saving grace that is in Jesus Christ and came to Him for healing of their souls. None has left the feet of Jesus disappointed, for the grace is for all who will receive it.

I first came to know of this marvelous and saving grace in April, 1971, at a Scripture Union conference. It was the day I accepted Jesus Christ into my life. I had heard of the new birth a few months earlier. Having grown up in a nominal Christian family, I immediately wanted this experience. However, one question remained: I was not quite sure Christ really existed.

If He did not exist, how could I accept Him into my life.? I was not ready to expose my life to such absurdity. But the possibility of going to hell after death forced me to settle this question once and for all. Yet, I could not deny the assurance these born-again Christians around me were having. I was on the brink of despair when I came to this conference. But then, God in His great mercy was there to meet me and to help me get over my unbelief.

One morning, after the preacher had given the invitation to accept Christ, I made a decision not to get up from my seat until I had settled the question of my salvation. A few minutes passed, and still nothing happened. Soon, a brother approached me and asked what was wrong. After I told him my problem, he called another brother and they took me to a room away from the noise of the auditorium. In the course of our discussion, I mentioned the church I had joined three years earlier. They recognized that church to be false and pointed out Scriptures that opposed its doctrines. Scales fell from my eyes as I realized my error. From then on, the Word of God could gain free entrance into my heart.

They then presented the simple message of salvation. They discussed some of the sins in the Bible. I had always prided myself in being a moral girl. But as I sat in that room, I came under the searching light of the Holy Spirit. I saw myself, not just as a sinner, but as the greatest sinner in the world.

Tears poured from my eyes as I confessed my sin. I told the Lord that I was sorry for my sin, and if He really existed, He should please come to my heart. After the prayers I opened my eyes. One of the brothers asked me if I was sure Christ had come into my heart. I said yes, not because I was certain that Christ had come into my heart, but because I knew I had to respond in faith. After all, He had promised that He would not reject anyone who would come to Him.

As soon as I made this positive confession, immediately heaven opened. A joy and peace to which I was a stranger flooded my heart. Christ became a real Person to me. I knew I was a child of God now, and my name had been written in heaven. I left the room still unable to contain the exuberance of my heart. I ran straight to my room singing the song I was unable to sing before:

Blessed assurance, Jesus is mine

Oh, what a foretaste of glory divine

Heir of salvation, purchase of God

Born of His Spirit, washed in His blood.

This is my story, this is my song

Praising my Savior all the day long;

This is my story, this is my song

Praising my Savior all the day long.

This grace was to continue with me throughout my Christian life.

I took my Christian life seriously. In 1978, after an incident, I began to memorize the Scriptures on a daily basis. It was the beginning of a new dimension for me.

After writing down Scriptures on a particular topic I would memorize them. This practice took me to a height in my Christian life that I never thought possible.

I soon discovered that I could hear God much clearer. Visions and dreams of the Lord became frequent. I would find myself in dreams sitting at the Lord's feet as He exposed Scriptures to me. At other times He would tell me of the sins in my life and command me to run from them.

The topic of grace was one of my favorites as I meditated on its power. I became very sensitive to the voice of the Holy Spirit and the Lord alerted me to mistakes I had made. The joy that accompanied the memorization of the Word was unspeakable. My prayer life, needless to say, was enriched.

I did not allow my marriage to disturb my prayer life. When the children had gone to bed at seven and my house chores were over, I would start my two-or three-hour quiet time. That was the grace of God. The grace that saved me on that memorable day in 1971 was the same grace that kept me through my marriage and after the accident.

Chapter

8

The Lord Visited Me

Before the accident I fasted once a week, and this discipline had richly blessed me. However, after the accident I found myself unable to fast. One Sunday, during the service at Christ For The Nations, the Lord told me to go on a seven day fast, and on the fourth or the fifth day, He would reveal Himself to me.

I began the fast the following day. Unfortunately, by 3 p.m. I was exhausted. I could not continue with the fast, and so I broke it. As I was praying two days later, the Lord once again said that He would reveal Himself to me in the next day or two. I was surprised for I had not kept the fast and had assumed that the Lord would not appear to me. I had limited His grace.

I clung to the promise of the Lord, and I eagerly awaited the revelation. Two nights later I was awakened at 1.30a.m. I felt a powerful oppressive spirit in the room. I opened my eyes, thinking it was the Lord since I had been waiting for His visitation. I was wrong.

Instead, I heard a voice which belonged to the devil tell me that it was he, and not the Lord, who had come. Suddenly, a force began to oppress me. At first I was confused, then I began to call on the name of Jesus. After calling His name six or eight times, I began pleading the blood of Jesus. I repeated "the Blood of Jesus" three times; then, I was free again.

I sat upright in my bed. This could not be, I thought. I was expecting to see the Lord, but the opposite had happened. I was still confused when the whole room became charged with the presence of the Lord Jesus Christ.

The next moment I was in another world. This world was very different from our physical world. It had a tone of permanency to it.

I later remembered that the Apostle Paul had also remarked that the things that are seen are temporal, but the things that are not seen are eternal. I sensed many demons around, but the Lord Jesus seemed to tower above all else. He was so tall that He seemed to go, from below this earth, through it and above it. And then the Lord started to speak to me. For about two hours He spoke. He told me He was going to teach me about demons. I do not remember the order in which they came. However, I still remember the points He showed me.

First the Lord taught me the power of united prayer. He referred me to Deuteronomy 32:30 that talks about one chasing a thousand but two chasing ten thousand. And then the Lord referred to my own experience in life concerning the power of agreement. I have discovered that when I wanted to receive a message from the Lord and I found myself unable to, I could call a Christian to agree with me and the message would come.

Contrary to my belief, the Lord told me that it was not He withholding the message from me, but the demons in the heavenlies intercepting it. However, when a Christian agrees with me, uniting his force with mine, a greater power is released to disband these demons.

The second point was about the power of speaking in tongues. I was taught by the Lord that speaking in tongues on certain occasions defeats demons in the spiritual world. In other words, it was a weapon of warfare. Again, I was reminded of how when I speak in tongues I hear the Lord's voice. The Bible says in 1 Corinthians 14:2 that when we speak in tongues, we speak mysteries to God. God knows all things, so He can direct our prayers aright. When we speak in tongues, it may be praise, prayer, or even thwarting the purposes of the devil: it all depends on the leading of the Holy Spirit.

Next, the Lord told me that His name received power because He came as a human being. He did not invade the world as demons do invading people's body. Instead, He came as a human being, born of a woman, and grew up in the normal way. Thus, as a bona fide citizen of the earth. He could receive this authority from the Father.

A year before, when Charles Capps taught this truth I had disagreed with Him. Now, here I was digesting the same truth, from the Lord. I had to believe. I was given Matthew 28:18 which says "All power is given unto me in heaven and in earth.

His greatest lesson to centered around an obscure verse in Colossians. It was a verse I had read several times that did not mean much to me, Colossians 2:15; "And having spoiled principalities and powers, he made a shew of them openly, triumphing over them in it." This verse was set in bold relief in this spiritual world. The Lord did not expatiate the verse in so many words, for the impact of the verse on me was great. It was so big it filled the atmosphere. The demons shuddered and trembled at the truth of the verse.

Again, I remember times when I am in spiritual combat and, when I mention the blood of Jesus there is victory. Demons have to fear the blood of Jesus, for the blood was shed when He defeated them on the cross.

This concluded my teaching session with the Lord, and needless to say, I was richly blessed.

One afternoon as I prayed, I began to hear the voice of the Lord again. He told me that at the time of the accident He had filled the inside of the car with His presence as my family was dying. He had not abandoned them, but was there with them until their last breath. No wonder I felt such serenity in the car that day!

Then, the Lord asked me if I wanted Him to tell me how they had died. I objected, afraid of being hurt. On second thought, I knew the Lord would not tell me anything that what could harm me. And so, thrusting myself on His goodness I asked Him to tell me.

He then told me it was suffocation that had killed them, not the fire. What comfort became mine in that instant! I had thought they suffered terrible burning, while in fact they had died of suffocation. No wonder my daughter had cried three times and then became silent.

Another evening, during my devotions, the Lord fulfilled the promise He gave to me in Nigeria. After I had seen the vision of Johnny in a transparent white gown playing a musical instrument, the Lord had promised me that He would give me an even greater vision about their state. I had often wondered what could be greater.

As I prayed on my knees, the Lord gave me a vision of the glorious Homegoing of my family. When they got to the heavenly portals, celebration had attended them.

It was like a royal welcome, only it was far greater than the glamor and honor given to an earthly king. Words are inadequate to capture this scene. Multitudes of beings, whom I believe to be angels, and saints welcomed them to their eternal rest. The honor they received was indescribable.

It was a brief vision, yet I caught its splendor. I got up from my knees with an unspeakable joy, praising God. I wondered why I had to continue to grieve for them. I began to share in the joy that had become theirs. And any time I remembered this vision months later, my heart would be comforted.

No, death cannot reign. Separation is not the final cause. Jesus, your Life has overcome death and hell. I await the moment when, in God's good time, I draw my last breath, and my eyes close in death. And I travel to worlds unknown, headed for my eternal destiny with the One who died and paved the way with His precious blood. No wonder the apostle had admonished us not to sorrow like those who do not have hope!

One day, the Lord told me I was leaving Christ For The Nations soon. I was surprised. I hate changes. Once I discover that something works, I stick to it. I had come to this school in obedience to the Lord and now, I did not want to leave. I told Him I was ready to follow His will and asked Him to speak and to lead me through His providence. I knew circumstances had to literally take me from this institution.

In December, the Lord told me to go and visit a Nigerian who was attending Oral Roberts University, in Tulsa, Oklahoma. God would use him to tell me what to do next. I obeyed the heavenly injunction and went to Tulsa.

He and his wife received me cordially. Of course, I did not disclose the reason for my visit. I simply told them I was led to visit them. After a few days, this brother offhandedly suggested that I should transfer to Oral Roberts University. He proceeded to tell me of the advantages attached to this God-ordained institution. I decided to pray about it. Yes, it was the Lord's will. I applied and was admitted to study for my Masters in Theology.

Chapter

9

My Inner Healing at Oral Roberts University

My first semester at ORU was filled with mixed emotions. I was greatly blessed and encouraged to see highly educated men talk freely of their charismatic experiences. They were not embarrassed to talk of their encounters with God.

I also learned a lot about the revealed Word- the Bible. One of the courses which I took, "Biblical Authority" taught by Dr. Larry Hart, exposed me to the tension surrounding the infallibility of the Scriptures. This course convinced me that the Bible we hold in our hands is truly the Infallible Word of God to man. Despite the attacks that had been launched against it through the ages, it has remained victorious.

The Bible took on a higher and greater meaning. Previously, I had simply believed the Bible to be the Word of God to man. Now, I knew more objectively why it is so. I could now give the reason for such conviction, in addition to my own experience. From then on, I was to dwell on it and read it with deeper reverence and appreciation; it was to become my rock and my strength.

It was like finding the pearl of great price. The prophet Jeremiah aptly described it when he said *"Thy words were found, and I did eat them and thy word became to me the joy and the rejoicing of mine heart."* [Jeremiah.15:16]

The courses I took at ORU were not merely intellectual exercises, but they were spiritually refreshing as well. However, I was faced with a great concern. Inside I had great joy, but my concentration span was very short. My mind could simply wander, contrary to my will. I could not look at people straight in the eye without losing my concentration. I could not remember the next sentence. I found myself struggling to follow through with my thoughts. My frustration knew no bounds. I later realized it was the effect of the concussion I had at the time of the accident for which I had received no treatment.

I knew could not withdraw from the seminary. God had called me there and God would see me thorough. Prayers were offered on my behalf. There was a time when it looked as though I was improving - but it was short-lived due to continued academic and financial pressure.

One day, I heard a knock at my door. It was Beverley Jones, a fellow seminarian with a major in Christian counseling. I had seen her but we seldom spoke. I was surprised to find her at my door. She told me she had a message from a friend to me, so I invited her in. Soon we were talking.

I told her I was going back to Nigeria in September and coming back the following year for my graduation; I planned to then take my remaining course during the summer. This would save me some money. She looked at me and said, "You are not ready to go back to Nigeria until you first process the grief out of your system." I remember being struck by her audacity. She said she would counsel me without charge.

We scheduled two sessions a week. After three or four counseling sessions, I was healed. My concentration was greatly improved, my nervousness was minimized. I was amazed at this recovery. Beverley was to become my close friend and confidante from then on. I realized the great gift God has given her, as have many people who have testified to this gift in her life. My gratitude goes beyond Beverley. It goes to the Almighty God, who in His mercy and wisdom sent her along my path.

Chapter

10

Forgiveness

Is there room in my heart to forgive the man who killed my family in their prime? Does he de serve my love, my sympathy, or even my consideration? Are there some criteria he must meet before I bestow my forgiveness on him? These were the questions with which I had wrestled.

Had someone asked me two days after the accident if I had truly forgiven this man, swift would have been my response: I had forgiven him. Accidents must happen, and since accidents are not voluntary, forgiveness on my part was reasonable, I had thought he had hit our car by accident.

This assumption was, however, shattered when a week after the accident, I read in the newspaper that the young man was legally drunk at the time. Anger welled up inside me. Their deaths could have been avoided. My family could have been alive but for him. It was his drinking problem that deprived me of my family. It was his drinking problem that obliterated all the dreams Johnny and I had had about our future.

Yes, it was his drinking problem that plunged my family into an early grave, that denied my children to reach adulthood and to be something in life. My husband left behind him no offspring to carry on his name. The dream of having grandchildren through my children has vanished. I had to start raising a new family-all because of one man's drinking problem.

Hatred for this man who had wreaked so much havoc was finding its way into my heart. Almost immediately, the Lord stopped me in my track. I realized I dared not but forgive. Unforgiveness must not lurk in my heart. I feared God too much to nurse this spirit. I also feared for myself.

I knew in my heart that my life was dependent on the mercy of God. Only the mercy of God was keeping my mind intact. I could not sacrifice my mental health for anything in the world, not even for the natural hatred this man deserved. And so, with the help of God, I stopped this unforgiving spirit from making its nest in · my heart.

However, it was not until two years later that I released him. It was not because I did not want to forgive him totally, but because I did not even know I had not forgiven. I did know, however, that I did not want to meet him. Although we had been transported in the same ambulance to St. Joseph's Hospital, I had not turned to see who it was, due to the pain in my back. Besides, I had not yet known the cause of the accident.

For almost two years, I did not want to meet this man for fear of being hurt, and also for fear of reliving the accident. He had already done the damage; I had forgiven him, and that brought the issue to a rest, I thought. But I did not realize that unforgiveness, in the form of apathy, was embedded in my heart.

I was greatly wounded when, eight months after the accident, my lawyer gave me some very disturbing news. The police had caught this young man while driving intoxicated. I felt cheated. The death of my loved ones was not even enough to teach this man that drinking and driving do not belong together.

Without hesitation on my part, I told the lawyer to withdraw the plea of leniency I had requested from the state on his behalf. He was a hazard to society, and he should be locked away where he could no longer constitute danger to the public-at-large. Once again, the seed of bitterness was sown and continued to germinate in the recess of my heart, yet I did not know it. How deceitful the heart!

His trial was to come up on the first of April - exactly a year after the accident. By now, honestly I did not care what would become of him in this trial. I did not care if he was alive or dead. Why should I waste my thoughts on him?

A couple of days after the trial, his probation officer called and told me that the state had found him guilty of involuntary manslaughter. She was conducting a presentence investigation, and she wanted to know the impact of the accident on me. Since I did not want the law to be too hard on him, I simply told her about my poor mental state.

Three weeks later, the telephone rang. It was a news reporter from Plattecity who had been following my case. He told me the young man had just received a four-year imprisonment and he asked for my comments. I told him his imprisonment would not bring my family back to life, but I hoped that this would teach the public at large about drinking and driving.

I asked the news reporter to send me the article. He acquiesced, and I received it three days later. Toward the end of the article, I read that some fifty members of that area had signed a petition that the man should receive a probation instead of imprisonment. Once again, anger welled up inside me, but I did not allow it to perturb me. I was too hurt to allow my thoughts to dwell on it. The probation officer called me later and told me the young man would be eligible for parole in eighteen months.

It was not until another ten months later that the Lord used Beverley Jones to bring out this unforgiveness in my heart. During counseling, Beverley probed me about my reaction to the boy. I tried to convince her that I had truly forgiven him. But she noticed the hollowness of my confession, and pointed out that my apathy denoted lack of forgiveness.

Suddenly, as if scales fell from my eyes, I realized that I had been burying the ill feelings; I had not released him. And so I began to confess aloud "James, you are forgiven, I forgive you, in Jesus' name." Soon, I began to experience the joy of forgiving others, as Christ has forgiven me.

Now, I am ready to meet him. I can smile at him, knowing that the past is behind. I can look at him now as if he has never done anything wrong. Two years after the accident, my lawyer told me this young man was very repentant and was engaged to be married. I am glad for him, and I hope that he will not allow his own remorse to stand in the way of his happiness.

Forgiveness is not easy. Those who are victims of heinous crimes will bear witness to this truth. However, forgiveness is vital in our relationship with God. Forgiveness encompasses both the vertical and horizontal dimensions. Both are important in our communion with

God. The Bible is replete with cases of forgiveness, both from above and from below.

Adam and Eve committed a high treason against God. This was the beginning of the human tragedy. Sin became the gulf that separated us from God, and the only remedy was forgiveness. Forgiveness of our sins from the God of justice became the central issue. Would God forgive or would He damn us? If He damned us, He would be justified, for we well deserved it.

His was the choice. God, however, in His infinite mercy chose to forgive us and proceeded to outline the terms of forgiveness.

The apex of divine forgiveness was the gift of His sinless Son. Whereas in the Old Testament the blood of a lamb was the blood that must wipe away sins, in the New Testament the focus shifted. The blood of Christ became the all-sufficient blood that can eradicate the blackest sin. No sin is too great to escape its power. Once shed, the blood is available for all eternity, What sublime love!

David experienced divine forgiveness in the Old Covenant. *"Bless the Lord, O my soul, and all that is within me, bless His holy name...who forgiveth all thy iniquities"* (Psalms 103). Yes, all his sins, secret and open, known and unknown, were pardoned through God's mercy. Now, he could say, *"Blessed is he whose transgression is forgiven, whose sin is covered!"* (Ps 32:1)

Isaiah was another mouthpiece of God. God is ready to forgive iniquities no matter how great the offense. If the sinner repents, He will pardon. Isaiah 1:18 says "Come now, and let us reason together, saith the Lord: though your sins be as scarlet, they shall be as white as snow; though they be red like crimson, they shall be as wool."

In the New Covenant, Zacchaeus experienced the forgiveness of Christ. He was an outcast, extortioner, one who had betrayed his own people. His love of money led him to join forces with the Roman government to levy taxes on the Jews. But when Jesus came his sins, though great were forgiven. That

was the mission of Christ to reconcile men and women to God through the forgiveness of their sins.

The thief on the cross, a criminal of the deepest dye, one that deserved to die on the cross, also received this forgiveness. In his last hour, he turned to Christ, and asked Him to remember him in the Kingdom of God. In a moment, the transaction was done. His sins were blotted out as though they did not exist. His open sins, as well as his secret sins, were forgiven. What a glorious event!

Christ came to call sinners to repentance. Upon their repentance and confession of their sins to God, all their sins will be remembered no more.

"Who is a God like unto thee that pardonneth iniq-

uity and passeth by the transgression of the remnant of His heritage? He retaineth His anger for ever, because He delighteth in mercy." (Micah 7:18)

Now God turns to us and asks us to follow in His footsteps by forgiving others. In fact, it is a prerequisite to receiving pardon for our own sins. Jesus emphatically said that if we do not forgive others, we cannot expect divine forgiveness. Yet, He has not left us to forgive in our own strength. He wants us to receive His enablement to forgive. We must be willing. It is a decision that we must make. Will you forgive that person in your life? Please do it, and do it now!

Chapter

11

The Secret of My Strength.

People often ask me the secret of my strength. They ask me how I am able to cope with life after the loss of my family. My response is that many factors contribute to this inner strength. Without a doubt, the grace of God is the number one factor that has carried me thus far, and the same grace, I am convinced, will see me through.

God is faithful and will do His part. However, He has outlined some principles in the written Word by which we can be strong in the grace of our Lord Jesus Christ. Paul admonished Timothy to be strong in this grace that knows no bounds.

In the early days, I found praise to be of great help. Praise and worship brought me closer to God than any other thing. Miracles of my emotional healing took place as I praised God. It was as I praised God on the day of the funeral, both in my apartment and in the cemetery, that I sensed the presence of God in a unique way. I experienced what goes on in heaven - the continuous praise of God. It was, as I praised God, that I was given the vision of my departed husband in his glory.

The Scripture says that God inhabits the praises of His children. He is seeking people who will worship Him in spirit and in truth. This truth shows that praise has a unique place in the heart of God. David, the man who knew the heart of God, praised Him. With what zeal did he praise the Almighty! He purposed in his heart that he would praise God seven times a day. No wonder he was called a man after God's own heart.

If we want God's will to be done here, as it is done in heaven, then we must praise God. It is only as God's will is done in our heart, that we experience heaven on earth.

Secondly, after a few months, I began to spend a lot of time in communion with God. Little intercession was done. I was too emotionally wrung dry to take on others' problems. I simply praised and communed with God. This time was a resting place where I could behold the face of the Lord continually, seldom asking for anything other than to know Him more. If I asked Him for anything, it was to know Him more.

You see I had everything I could hope for. Since

God is my Refuge and help I became fulfilled. Yes, my family was gone; yet, I was comforted, happy and on top of the world. The secret of this wholesomeness is fellowship with God. I discovered that ultimate satisfaction and fulfillment can come from the One who made us.

Thirdly, holiness played a vital role in my life. The Lord had emphasized this truth to me several times. I did not want to do things that would block my relationship with God. I could not afford to play with sin. I became acutely aware of its impact on my life.

The Bible says that without holiness no man shall see the Lord. If I was to abide in His holy hill, then I must keep myself unspotted from the world. The Lord taught me the importance of holiness in a vision. He told me to flee the least appearance of sin. I must run from it. If God had to limit Himself to taking on human flesh to save us from sin, then we too must take this matter of sin seriously.

By far, the greatest secret of my life is the Word of God. I spent a great deal of my time not merely reading it, but also memorizing it. The ultimate goal was not to be able to quote it. I had discovered, before the accident, the power of memorization of the Word. When I rehearsed these Scriptures with my mouth, I found myself meditating on it. And the presence of the Holy Spirit would fill my spirit.

Before the accident, it got to the point that, when I started to rehearse these verses, my heart would begin to burn. I would not dare continue, simply laying my Bible aside to worship God. Such was the effect of the Word on me. The Lord was later to tell me the Word was cleansing my soul. Jesus said *"You are made clean by the Word which I have spoken to you."* (John 15:3)

The Bible thus became the greatest book in the whole word to me. The joy I experienced, as I memorized and meditated on it is indescribable. My whole body would be filled with joy. My happiness was no longer depended on my circumstances, but on the eternal Word which abides forever. I was to regard the Word to be of greater value to me than my food, sacrificing my sleep and food rather than to go without it. Often, I would weep in gratitude to God for His revealed Word.

Praise God, we have access to this Word! There is much life in its pages. Its message is deathless, its commands changeless, and its truth is timeless. Jesus, who is our Life, pledges His personal presence in His Word for He Himself said, *"The words that I speak to you, they are spirit and they are life"* (John 6:63). This Word is the basis of our salvation, and it is obvious that it is the same Word that can take us through our Christian journey here on earth.

This Word has imparted life where death reigns. *"Lazarus, come forth"* bears witness to its life-giving power (John 11:43). It has not lost its ancient power, as it continues to impart life. All over the world, wherever this gospel is preached, the life of God is imparted to its hearers.

The Word is also the light. I discovered that it brightens my view of God. It sensitizes my spirit to God. I could hear Him better after meditating on His words. In its pages lie the answer to our questions. Men and women down through the ages have tried to destroy it, but to no avail, for no darkness can overcome this book which is the light of the world. It is the book for all occasions.

The brokenhearted soul has found solace as he meditates on it, and there the thirsty has received the water of life. The hungry soul has been fed to the full, and the questioner has found the solution to his problem. The bereaved and the comfortless have received comfort. The weak has been made strong and the poor has been invited to partake on the unsearchable riches in Christ.

The sages have had to lay aside their earthly wisdom at the feet of Jesus, as they lay claim to the true wisdom and true knowledge of God. The troubled soul has found peace that passes all understanding, and the suicidal has found the Prince of Life within its pages.

The Word is so powerful that it holds the universe in its place, *"upholding all things by the word of His power"* (Hebrews 1:3). God has spoken and the elements must obey. God spoke to the waves of the sea: *"Hitherto shalt thou come but no further; and here shall thy proud waves be stayed"* (Jer 5:22). No wonder the mighty oceans have not flooded the earth!

Jesus Christ, the Word that became flesh, spoke to the turbulent sea and it obeyed Him. Such is the power of the Word. It will stand amidst the turbulence of life. It will stand when all seems to fail. Its power to change any circumstance in life has not changed.

Little wonder it has been the focus of the attack of the devil and his children. Men and women have sought to get rid of the Bible, and where they have failed, they have sought to discredit its message. But they forgot that they were kicking against God and their efforts were doomed for failure.

God is watching over his Word to perform it and I daresay, to preserve it. "Heaven and earth will pass away but My word will not pass away." These men have come and gone; Nero, Darwin, Voltaire and others who would have deprived us of the availability of the Word and its message are no more here. They had predicted the extermination of the Bible, but it was they, as the Bible predicted, that passed away. Unfortunately, others have followed suit, including liberal theologians, sad to say, who are trying to disprove the infallibility of the Scriptures. Like their predecessors, they too must pass away. But the Bible cannot pass away, neither can it be forgotten. It has been established for all generations.

Indeed, men and women down through the ages

have turned to it for answers to life's problems and they have not been disappointed as they approach it with faith, for the Bible ministers to the soul like no other book. It is food to our hungry soul. No other book can satisfy the deepest longing of our inner being. Only the Bible, God's Word to man, has passed the test.

When the good news was first preached by Jesus Christ, it set people free from eternal damnation. This same Word that brought freedom to those people, was equally effective in the days that followed. In a single day, the day of Pentecost, 3,000 souls were birthed into the Kingdom of God as Peter preached the same simple message. Peter later wrote *"But the Word of God abides forever; And this is the word which preached to you"* (1 Peter. 1:25)

The same gospel is still being preached; it is producing the same result because it is the Word of God that cannot die. Its power is eternal. Young and old alike in our generation are being born again through the Word, and the number is in the ascendancy. Doctors, lawyers, university professors, illiterates, cab drivers, carpenters, all rub shoulders at the feet of the Bible, where all alike find peace.

Blessings accrue for all who would diligently search its pages and follow its prescription. If we did away with it, our world would be driven to a chaos where the moral decay would spell the doom of man. Oh, that men would take refuge in the written Word of God! Read it to be wise. Read it to be enlightened in the true knowledge of God.

Read it again and again, Chew on it, feast on it, dine on it and you will discover the meaning of life — life in its abundance.

Chapter

12

Conclusion

W hat do I think of this tragedy? To say that I know the whole purpose of God in this accident, would be presumptuous. God is not a "thing" and therefore cannot be put in a box. Our human reasoning and logic cannot begin to fathom the great mind of God. His wisdom and His judgment go beyond our human understanding.

Misfortunes have often been attributed to the devil. The Bible teaches that the thief, which is the devil, has a three-fold mission. He came to steal, to kill, and to destroy. But Jesus came to destroy the works of the devil. Instead of death, He came to give life, and life in its abundance. This is the truth of the Scriptures.

However, to conjecture that all "misfortunes" are the deeds of the sovereign evil one is to be biblically ignorant. Exceptions are recorded in the Scriptures to guide us. Pious men and women, in biblical times and through the ages to the present times, have had mishaps in their lives. This fact cannot be denied.

Job was a classic case and his is a familiar story. Job loved God passionately. God Himself took pride in Job and testified that Job was a perfect man. Job lived an upright life and hated sin with an intensity that many Christians today cannot parallel. He did not have the law of Moses, but the law of his God was engraved in his heart. Job had indeed won divine favor. If there ever was a man who should not suffer, it was Job.

Job became a battleground. The devil had contested Job's motivation for serving God, and wanted to test Job to the core of his being. The devil's wish was that Job would deny his faith and sin against the Almighty. God allowed Satan to tempt Job, as the Bible records. It was not God who inflicted the sufferings, but He did allow them for a purpose. For reasons beyond Job's knowledge or even understanding, he went through this difficult time. But God did not leave Job during his trials and temptations, He was there to strengthen and comfort him.

As soon as Job received bad news, he knew where to turn. He went straight into the presence of God and worshiped Him. Job knew his God to be good, not capricious like the gods of the heathen. No wonder he said, *"Though he slay, me yet will I trust him...I shall come forth as gold"* (Job 13:15a; 23:10b)

Job had passed the initial test; this grace was to continue to strengthen him. Finally, he did come out of the fire as gold. What the devil meant for evil, God changed for good. That is our God - the God whose heart is full of love. The Bible states that the last days of Job were better than the first.

The Bible records only a few cases in which God allowed these mishaps to occur to His children for a purpose. The apostle Paul was another example. Paul prayed that the "thorns" would be removed. In the past, God had answered Paul's prayers positively. But this time, God said He was allowing this "thorn" for a reason. It was an exception, not a general rule. God wanted Paul to know His grace in a new dimension, that is, in Paul's weakness (2Corinthians 12:9). This is the plain truth of the Bible.

The crucial question arises: Is it God's will each time a mishap befalls a Christian? The Bible repudiates this notion. God is a good God. The Bible is replete with accounts of the goodness of God. The thoughts God has for us, the Scriptures declare, are thoughts of good and not of evil.

However, there are times when we are not sensitive to the voice of the Holy Spirit alerting us to an impending danger. In these cases, the suffering was not the will of God. Even so, nothing takes God by surprise and He can make some good come out of it. You see, God is not only omnipotent, He is equally omnicompetent. Glory be to His holy Name!

When this accident occurred, I had to search myself for any hidden sin. Why was it not revealed to me the afternoon we had travelled? After all, the Lord had spoken to me of my trip to Nigeria. Did I fail in some area of my life? But the Lord told me specifically that it was not because of any sin in my life that my family was snatched away, neither was I spared because of my righteousness. Johnny had finished his job and it was time for him to go home. He has now heard the words "Well done, good and faithful servant, enter thou into the joy of your master." This was a revelation the Lord gave me.

How about the children? Had they finished their work? Did they even start their earthly work? This is where my reason fails and my logic ends. Temple had just turned eight on the eve of the accident. The twins were not yet three. Why did they have to die? How could the loss of a husband and children be for the good of a wife and a mother? Oh, how I wish I had the answer in the palm of my hand!

Again, why was I spared and in such a miraculous

way? Was I more innocent than the children who had died? It was not a human hand that pulled me out of the car, lest I should be considered "lucky". God sent two angels to rescue me from the flames. The angels could have, saved the rest without difficulty, but they did not.

The fact that God sent these angels to rescue me demonstrates that it is God who is sovereign, not the defeated devil. Jesus Christ is still in control. Praise God, He is still the God of the whole earth, for all authority in heaven and earth is His. My comfort does not lie in the fact that the devil did it. My comfort lies in the knowledge that God is still in the heavens, and that I am His child. In this assurance I take my repose.

A TRIBUTE TO MY DEPARTED FAMILY.

Darlings,

As I write this, it is now three years since you have gone to your eternal rest. It is also two years that your eternal destiny has been fixed in God. My consolation rests in the knowledge that you settled the question of your salvation here on earth. I have no drop of worry about your eternal estate, for I know you are at the feet of the Master.

You have now become citizens of heaven where all around is peaceful and serene. The earthly turbulence is a thing of the past. Tears and sorrows are gone for ever and ever. The peace, that final peace, which belongs only to the Redeemed in heaven, has become yours.

The power of temptation is broken. The time of struggling with the world, the flesh, and the devil is over. Your holiness is completed, your sanctification eternal.

And the joy that accompanies such holiness is now yours to possess.

Angels are now your companions. The saints are now your friends as together, you tread the streets of gold. Holiness is now your environment. The Word of God, which you held in your hands while in this world, is as powerful as ever. The things you had to believe on earth are now what your eyes can behold. You know the complete reality of the Word now as you continue trusting in its eternal power.

Above all, you have seen the Master face to face. You have touched Him. You have seen those marks of crucifixion — the marks you did not see here on earth, but which you believed anyway. You have seen those eternal marks on His hands and on His feet that will remind you forever of what it took the Lord of Glory to bring you there.

Praises of Him who died for you, now fill your lips. You can continue to worship God in spirit and in truth, as you did here on earth. Only now, it is with a clearer vision, purer insight and greater love. What joy and peace must be yours now. What gratitude for the Savior must now be in your hearts.

You can look back to your earthly life and thank your Redeemer for bringing you into His fold. You have fought the fight; you have run the race. Now, you are eligible citizens of heaven, all because Jesus died and rose again. Death no longer holds terror. Because Jesus lives we too have eternal life.

As for me, I must continue the works of the Master here on earth. I must complete the task He has given me to do. When my earthly work is done we shall meet again, be it in heaven or in the sky. Keep on in your eternal rest my dears, my joy, my crown until you bid me welcome at the heavenly portals. Then, we shall meet to part no more.

In the meantime, we shall continue to worship the same Redeemer. Space and time will not keep us from praising the One who died that we might live. And throughout eternity will we express our deepest gratitude to the One who set us free from spiritual poverty, who healed our broken hearts, and above all reconciled us to His God.

Indeed, we can say, "Thank you, Jesus, for translating us from the kingdom of darkness to the Kingdom of Light. How we have failed you many times, but Your love abides still. We do appreciate You. We love You. We worship You, and we shall continue to praise You as long as eternity shall last."

Jesus knows all, and we can lay everything at the feet of Him who holds the whole world in His hand.

Our God still reigns. He is still sovereign. And yes, He still is the Lord.

A WORD TO THE UNSAVED

This is not a word of man to you, penned though it may be by a human hand. It is the Word of the Almighty to you. Do not think twice that you are reading this book by chance. God in His providence has bought this book along your path.

If you have not given your life to Christ, this is the time to do it. Do not wait till tomorrow, for you do not know what tomorrow holds. For your own sake, you need to know what God has to tell you through the Scriptures.

You have sinned against the Holy God. *"For all have sinned and come short of the glory of God."* Romans 3:23. The holiness of God demands that you pay for it. "The soul that sinneth, it shall die" (Ezekiel 18:4)

You are therefore dead spiritually, although you are walking about in your physical body. This spiritual death, into which we are all born, must eventually lead to the eternal death, which is spending eternity in the lake of fire.

God saw our condition and, in His mercy and love, intervened. This He did by sending His only Son, Jesus Christ, to take away our sin and to die the death that held us in its grips. He became the "Lamb of God that taketh away the sin of the world." He was born into our world to die. That was His primary mission. The Son of God had to put on the human form, in order to defeat the devil, the author of sin, death, and human suffering.

As Jesus hung on the tree of Calvary, His blood was shed. This blood was the only means by which your sin and my sins can be wiped away, never to be remembered by God. The blood of Jesus became the bridge between God and man. There was no other way. No man could do this, no prophet could shed His blood, because he is also a sinner. The only one qualified was the sinless Son of God. What great love God had for man!

Now, what is your part in this plan? You must repent of your sins; both small and great, for they are all grievous before God. The sin of lying, fornication, drugs, backbiting, incest, witchcraft consulting, disobedience to parents, evil thoughts, and robbery are only a few of the long list. You know your sins, and so does God.

Find a secret place where you can concentrate, and

confess your sins to God. Tell Him you are sorry. Mean it.

Next, ask him to forgive you and to cleanse you by the blood of Jesus, His Son. Believe that He has. Jesus will not turn you away on account of your sins. No sin is too black, that cannot be wiped away. The blood of Jesus is enough to wipe away ALL sin, both great and small. It does not matter if you have killed six million people, or handed your soul over to the devil. The blood of Jesus is sufficient to cleanse you. Listen to the promise of God to all who dare to repent: "Though your sins be as scarlet, they shall be white as snow, though they be red like crimson they shall be as wool"

Thirdly, ask Christ to some into your heart. He has promised in His word, "Behold, I stand at he door, and knock: if any man hear my voice and open the door, I will come in to him,.." Revelation. 3:20.

Jesus is faithful to His Word. He is not a man to tell lies. If you sincerely ask Him to come to your heart, He will. He is eager to give you a new life and new zest for life. You will experience a life that you never dreamed possible.

Now, thank Him and share His new found joy with a friend.

Find a good Bible-preaching church. God will direct you to a good church if you ask Him. It is very important that you affiliate with other believers.

TRIUMPH PUBLISHERS
P. O. Box 690158,
Bronx, New York, 10469
Tel. (718) 652-7157

BOOKS BY TAI IKOMI

His Beauty For My Ashes

A heart-rending yet exhilarating account of a mother's and a wife's journey through one of life's bitterest tragedy. In a single day, she lost her husband and three children to a drunk driver. In this moving account, the author describes her struggles, the bitter feelings, the frustration, and how the Lord turned her ashes into beauty. Evelyn (Oral) Roberts, in her foreword wrote, *"Anyone who has gone through a tragedy and is having a struggle because of it should read this book."* You will be glad you did!   **$6.95**

The Flaming Sword

The Flaming Sword shares how hiding God's Word in your heart results in many benefits including: emotional healing, faith to believe God's promises, power to resist sin, renewed love for God and others etc. You will learn simple and practical ways to memorize and meditate on the Scripture that will transform the mediocre Christian into a spiritual giant.   **$6:95**

Dare To Be The Best Wife

A practical book on how a woman can be the wife of her husband's dream in the light of the Scriptures. Intensely practical, the book provides information on building a strong marriage that will bring joy and fulfillment. It is a book every wife, young and old should read periodically.

$5:95

Dare To Be the Best Husband

A practical book on how a man can meet the needs of the woman he married. It addresses the differences between the man and the woman, and the practical clues from God's Word that can lead to a strong and happy marriage. It is a book every husband, young and old, should read periodically.

$5:95

Singles: How To Recognize The Compatible Spouse

Should I or should I not marry this person? What are the criteria to base my decision on? These are questions "Singles: *How To Recognize The Compatible Spouse*" addresses. This book may save you from the wrong marriage. Great for counseling.

$6:95

Your Child: Surely Wonderful

Raising children is crucial to the future of your child. To love your child is instinctive; to train him is not. It has to be learned. Your Child: Surely Wonderful offers practical ways of raising a wonderful and healthy child, emotionally, academically and spiritually. Every parent must read this book.

$6:95

You Can Overcome Your Temptations

Temptation cannot be ignored. It is part and parcel of the Christian race. Practical clues from God's Word and Christian experience on how to overcome those besetting sins

that you have worked to hard so overcome. This book
may be your answer.   **$6:95**

Quiet Time With God

A consistent personal devotion is the path to spiritual
strength. Happy is the Christian who is taught from con-
version to have a daily Quiet Time. This book discusses
practical hints and the purpose of Quiet Time, its fruits as
well as its enemies! Quiet Time With God will encourage
and teach you to lead a healthy personal devotional life.

$6:95

The Virtue of Forgiveness

A Sequel To His Beauty For My Ashes Forgiveness holds
an important place in the word of God, so much so that it
features in the short model prayer of Jesus Christ. The Bible
is quite explicit about forgiveness. It does not only deal
with the command to forgive, but also supplies practical
steps to achieving it. This book brings out how the Christian can forgive the offender with the help of God. The
author draws from personal experience of how she for-
gave the young man who killed all her family on an inter-
state highway while driving intoxicated.   **$6:95**

The Source Of My Joy

Third Sequel To His Beauty For My Ashes. Everyone
wants joy. And it makes sense. It is compatible with our
nature. But unhappily, something or the other deprives us
of our joy. The book discusses practically how the Christian can be joyful all the time. It is the promise of our
heavenly Father. You will wonder why you ever lived a
day without the joy of the Lord in your heart. The author

shares from her experiences how she could maintain a joyful life even after the death of her husband and three children. **$5:95**

Strength In Crisis

Second Sequel To His Beauty For My Ashes. Trials are real, often packaged in mysteries that we cannot understand. Today we ask why Christians go through trials. We cry to God for answer. This book will examine this evasive subject in the light of God's Word. It will bring rescue to those in trial and peace to the troubled heart with the timeless message: You are not forgotten by God. **$8:95**

Made To Be Like Him

When God made man, He spelled out in clear terms the reason for his existence. And this purpose has not changed. Learn how to bear the image of God here on earth and fulfill your potential. *(Coming Soon)* **$5:95**

Renew Your Mind Through Bible Meditation

At the onset of Joshua's ministry, God told him to meditate on His Word. The reason, God stated, is to be able to obey God. The reason remains the same. Many more blessings are attached to Bible meditation. This Book examines these reasons and more importantly, how to get into the art of meditating on the Word of God. It is a task every Christian should and can do. Your life will not be the same. **$6.95**

Proverbs Analysis

Some Christians may find the Book of Proverbs hard to understand. But the book of Proverbs provides wonderful insights into daily living. Proverbs Analysis categorizes the proverbs of King Solomon into various themes such as: Advice To The Wife, Advice To The Husband, The Advantages Of Hard Word, The Fruit of the Fear of God, Friendship etc. Proverbs Analysis will open up a new world to you. You are now able to go directly to the particular subject you specifically need an answer for.   **$6:95**

Fifty Names Of God

God has given us names by which He may be addressed in the Bible. These names depict His character and personality. Over fifty names of God in Hebrew and in English (most of them unknown) with their Scriptures and references are provided. There is also a brief introduction on how the need to know the names of God and how to study and use them. Get ready to move to a realm where only those who know God can enjoy .   **$5.95**

ORDER FORM
Tai Ikomi
Triumph Publishing
P. O. Box 690158
Bronx, New York 10469
1-718-652-7157

Name: _____

Address _____

City _____ State _____

Zip _____ Phone ( ) _____

Qty	Title of Book	Price	Total

Volume Discounts on large Orders.
Allow 3-4 weeks Delivery

Shipping/Handling (10% of Retail) $3.00 minimum

Special Offer: If you order all the books, subtract 10% off the price!

Total